we are for
change

@What_we_are_for

#WeAreFor

we are for
change

Introduction

Modern politics seems to have become about division. Even in the time of a coalition government constant argument, elongated debate, filibustering and media points scoring now dominates the news headlines, with scandal and character attacks taking more column inches than progress and with dogma taking more air time than social development. Popularity contests get more attention than popular policy and the electorate are more interested in voting for singing and dance competitions than for political parties.

Politicians spend so much time fighting over issues and desperately trying to inform the electorate why their opposition are wrong and what they are against, they have forgotten to tell their voters what they are for. The truth is that there is more in life that unites us as a nation than divides us. Regardless of age, race, sex, colour, faith, cast, creed or political affiliation, if we were to focus on solving the problems rather than winning the debate, if we could generate more options, create more ideas and more political solutions, if we could find more common ground then we could make more progress in areas we can agree on and potentially help to improve the lives of the many sooner without having to negotiate, debate, argue or mandate.

So this is dedicated to those who are sick of soundbite politics, of policies boiled down to bullet points and to those who are sick of three point plans for our country. We deserve more than that. The problems that face us are bigger then a three point could ever present. They are bigger than bullet points and bigger than soundbites. This is for those who want to know more, who want to be a to be a part of the debate and who want to move forward. The better informed we are the more ideas we can generate ideas and the more we can work together to make our country a better place for our children and for our children's children.

For those who want to help find the solution, this is **What We Are For.**

we are for change

Contents

We Are For

	page		page
Society	4	Housing	28
Economy	6	Transport	29
Education	9	Culture & Sport	31
Health	12	Youth	32
Defence	15	Justice	33
Home Affairs	17	Policing & Correction	34
Business & Enterprise	19	Foreign Affairs	36
Work & Pensions	21	Europe & Immigration	37
Unemployment	22	Charity & Aid	39
Taxation	23	Environment	40
Benefits	25	Energy	41
Local Affairs	27	The Future	42

we are for
change

Society

We Are For

Freedom of Speech.

Equality regardless of age, race, colour, creed, sex, sexual orientation, political allegiance, religion, faith, accent, occupation, location, income, intellect or ability.

Governance of the people by representative elected from among the people.

Everyone having the right to vote in a democratic election to determine who represents them in governing.

Debate, both by those elected to govern and among the people.

Democracy and the right to decide for all people across the world.

All people of the world being free to determine their own fate.

Freeing the oppressed from fear and tyranny wherever they are in the world.

Governmental transparency

Standing up for those who are unable to stand up for themselves.

Helping those who do not have the means to help themselves.

Supporting all those who want democracy, the right to decide their fate and freedom of speech across the world.

All the people of the world living free.

The right to self determination.

The right to a life lived in peace and without fear of persecution, oppression or fear of suppression.

Freedom of assembly.

People with similar opinions coming together to give voice to an issue or belief.

People with similar opinions coming together to try and solve societies issues.

The rule of law.

The process of law to be determined by the elected representative of the people.

we are for
change

Restricting the power of the government and of the people's representatives.

The right to recall a representative of the people.

Our elected representatives representing the views of all of their constituents, not just those that voted for them.

Standing shoulder to shoulder with all those who share our ideas and need our support.

The right to protest our government and demonstrate our opposition to their policies.

Our fellow man, wherever they are around the globe. They are our neighbours and if they are in need we will support them.

Not letting politics get in the way of what we know to be morally right.

Supporting others to resolve their disputes.

The individual's right to privacy.

Making voting easier.

Multi-party politics.

Political parties being financed by their members.

Limits to individual and organisational donations to political parties and organisations that lobby our parliament.

Publishing lists of those who donate regularly and in large amounts to political parties or interest groups.

The provision of means tested free and subsidised child care.

Supporting new parents and new borns with care, advice and monitoring until school age.

Freedom, human rights and democracy.

National and local politics and political institutions with the power and ability to influence and improve the quality of our lives.

Political expenses being published for all to see.

All political expenses being over seen and approved by an independent body.

UK sovereignty and constitution.

we are for
change

Economy

We Are For

Free trade, across borders, across the world.

Determining our own economic future, free from ties to other people, organisations, companies or countries that have economies different to our own.

Our own currency.

Being able to support ourselves.

Exporting goods and services across the world.

Importing goods and services from around the world.

Exporting more than we import.

Thinking of new ways to encourage foreign investment into our country.

Thinking of ways to ensure we export more than we import.

Thinking to the future and then investing to get there.

Preparing our children for the future workplace better.

Blue sky thinking.

Leading the world in technology, engineering, design, creativity, finance, service provision, manufacturing and retail.

Removing the red tape of regulation to create markets that can move with consumer needs.

Helping our companies market themselves at home and abroad.

Providing a support and funding network for new entrepreneurs and developing organisations.

Ambition

The strategy to achieve it.

Protecting our domestic producers without protectionism, favouritism or tariffs, by helping them to be competitive.

Utilising more of our domestic products and services.

Fair competition between organisations, markets and economies.

Pushing new boundaries and forging new markets.

we are for change

Encouraging enterprise by taxing fairly.

Rewarding employment through tax incentives.

Investing in business and enterprise to generate economic prosperity and employment.

Being a leading member of the global economy.

Fair systems of regulation and punitive penalties to ensure a fair but competitive marketplace.

A budget in surplus

Paying off our national debt.

Not encumbering our children and our children's children with crippling national debt repayments.

Spending more on essential services than on debt repayments and interest.

Living within our means.

Investing budget surpluses into enterprise and economic growth.

Fair taxation for all individuals and organisations without loop holes.

Closing loop holes in taxation and back charging those who benefitted from them.

Investing budget surpluses into enterprise and economic growth.

Tax revenue recycling.

Capping borrowing as a percentage of GDP.

Reducing the burden of taxation on the lowest income earners.

Ensuring high earning individuals and organisation contribute fairly though taxation.

Strict fiscal and economic rules.

The national economy benefitting from the profits of organisations.

IMF and World Bank reform.

Enabling citizens to accumulate wealth.

Not punishing those who have accumulated wealth from passing it on to their children, families, loved ones or charities.

All positive contributions to our economy.

we are for
change

Preventing individuals and organisations from profiteering and exploiting the financially disadvantaged, impoverished or insolvent.

Creating a stable, industrially balanced economy.

Building economic momentum.

Public shared ownership of banks.

A people's bonus from bailed out banks.

More diverse forms of small business and home ownership credit.

Clear financial service regulation.

Affordable and backed credit for SME's.

Reducing industrial regulation and red tape.

Public bodies and private organisations working together.

Supporting innovative SME's with government contracts and challenges.

Low credit interest rates.

Controlled inflation.

Saving money through reducing bureaucracy

Leading the world in high tech manufacturing and exports.

Rewarding individual regular savers with improved interest rates.

Banning excessive borrowing rates on all forms of credit and loan.

Macroeconomic stability.

A balanced, diverse economy.

The separation and partition of personal savings and organisational investment banking.

Open markets.

Opening new markets for UK products and services.

UK sovereignty and constitution.

Maintaining British power over British economic, social, defence and government policies.

Leading the world Green Economy.

Taking back our fishing waters.

we are for
change

Education

We Are For

Free primary and secondary education for all children.

Preparing our children for the future workplace.

Encouraging our children to choose their own path.

Encouraging everyone to make a valuable contribution to society.

Teaching all to the best of their ability.

Teaching all children the essential subjects, knowledge and skills for the future economy and society to better equip them all to positively contribute to society.

Leading in healthcare education from primary school.

Minimum standards in maths, English and computing skills before a child can leave school.

Grants for university and college students from low income families who study in economically attractive courses.

Requiring university degrees and teaching qualifications from all teachers.

Free university education / paying down of student loans for all who become and remain state school teachers.

Leading sexual education in secondary schools.

Local businesses, organisations and individuals getting involved in education provision.

Utilising local experts to provide broader education and practical insight.

Assisting working parents through school opening hours.

State of the art building and equipment for all pupils.

University fees to vary based on means, course attractiveness and domestic vs. international qualifications.

Using new technology to improve and compliment learning and teaching.

De-regulating Universities and Colleges.

we are for
change

Standardised testing in core subjects.

Teaching our children how to solve everyday problems.

Teaching our children how to find the answer rather than giving it to them.

Learning and growing through discovery and development, experimentation and inquisition.

Challenging our children in different ways.

Relating classes to real life.

Leading in wealth education.

Encouraging discovery in the arts, music, reading and creativity.

Encouraging creativity and recognising diversity

Parental involvement in education and educational direction.

Continuing the classroom lesson at home not just through individual assignment.

Education being a privilege.

Identifying and encouraging talent.

Encouraging education until eighteen.

Parental responsibility and accountability for their child's behaviour and education.

Technology for all.

Setting minimum standards for the quality of our children's education.

Setting objective for our children's education.

Communities working with schools to support the development and education of our youth.

Business and industry working in communities to develop and create opportunities for our youth.

New industries and technology companies working with schools to inspire our children.

Publishing school standards and performance reviews.

Apprenticeships and vocational training as an alternative to continued education.

we are for
change

Extra funding for schools in deprived areas.

Involving local communities and enterprise in education.

Paying or subsidising university fees for those who become teachers in state schools.

Paying or subsidising tuition fees for those who change careers into teaching and other nationally essential careers.

Rewarding service personnel who switch to teaching after their military career ends.

Making it easier and more transparent to exclude and suspend pupils from schools.

Holding parents responsible for pupils who disrupt the education of others.

Innovation in teaching methods.

Minimum requirement in Maths, English and Computing before eligibility for Job Seekers Allowance or other unemployment benefit.

Encouraging business and educational collaboration and course development.

Encouraging and teaching healthy lifestyle education at school.

Challenging our children to be active.

Making time in every school day for active exercise.

Using our children to lead the country to be healthier.

Tackling inactivity and unbalanced diets as the root cause of obesity.

Teaching nutrition in school.

Supporting local sporting organisations and those who teach children to be healthier.

Ensuring the best teachers are in state and not private schools.

Minimum teaching standards and published school assessments.

All teachers to be degree educated in the subject they are teaching.

All teachers to spend time each year in state schools.

Encouraging business and further educational collaboration and product development.

we are for
change

Health

We Are For

Universal healthcare provision for all, free at the point of consumption, from cradle to grave.

Prevention before cure.

Leading with health, wellbeing, fitness and nutritional education in school.

24/7 access to healthcare.

The best & most efficient healthcare system in the world.

Investing in care givers.

Relieving the burden on the NHS through organisational private healthcare schemes.

Frontline services.

Clear demarcation of frontline services.

Investing in the root causes of our health issues not the end results.

Proactively targeting smoking, heart disease, obesity and other co-morbilities across the life time of our citizens.

Investing to be world leaders in new treatments, drugs and cures.

Whole person care across the health spectrum.

Investing in healthcare training for all professions and specialisms.

Cross party leadership of vital health service provisions.

Areas of specialism and widespread generalism.

Community based healthcare services.

Sharing patient information between services.

Investing in technology to reduce paperwork and care down time.

Migrants and visitors paying for NHS care through health insurance

Effective but non intrusive regulation and oversight.

Offsetting the costs of Alcohol, Drug and Smoking related preventable care through insurance or charging.

Free/subsidised University/College education for all essential, frontline and low band public health key workers.

we are for
change

Leading sexual health education in schools.

Easy access to medical services.

Easy access and close proximity to emergency and accidental medical services.

Putting patient care at the heart of the NHS.

Independent, voluntary and community healthcare provided within NHS standards.

Visibility of healthcare standards, performance, education and quality.

Doctors having the ability and finances to prescribe the drugs and treatment that patients need.

The Cancer Drugs Fund.

Patients' rights and minimum safety standards.

24/7 care within convenient requirement.

The highest standards of cleanliness.

A cancer treatment fund paid for from the profits of drug companies and pharmaceutical retailers.

Regular dental, visual and hearing check-ups for all.

Making it easier to get and fund necessary care including respite.

Recompensing carers.

Caring for our elderly, disabled and infirm in their own homes where possible.

Supporting and providing respite for both official and unofficial carers.

Providing local and national support networks for carers.

Providing training and support for both official & unofficial carers.

Putting patients safety and care quality not targets back at the heart of the NHS.

Those who can afford it having private health programs.

Ensuring all workers have access to an occupational healthcare scheme.

Polypharmacy.

Regional health strategies to combat the biggest health issues.

Free prescriptions for the long term sick, low income households, children and new mothers.

**we are for
change**

An NHS that aligns service and training.

An NHS that patients can trust at the point of use.

Transparency in treatment, care, quality and standards.

Pharmacists within primary care.

All doctors spending time in the NHS.

Longer post-natal care for all mothers.

Encouraging innovation and on-going training at all levels in the healthcare system.

Defence

We Are For

Securing our borders in the air, land and sea.

Protecting our citizens from all threats both foreign and domestic.

Protecting the weak from tyranny and oppression around the world.

Not shying away from what we know to be morally right.

Monitoring threats to our nation using all means necessary and appropriate.

Peace, harmony, stability and national freedom.

Utilising our military to maintain these things.

Peacekeeping and impartiality around the world.

The active conversation of peaceful nations.

Uniting against a common enemy.

Defeating the threat of global terrorism.

A standing army, navy, air force and security service.

Training and equipping our military for the needs of defending against modern threats and combat.

Modernisation.

Developing weapons, tactics and structures to combat modern threats.

Working with our allies.

Ensuring we are equipped to combat threats to our nation.

Negotiation and discussion as a first effort.

Exhausting negotiation and sanctions before taking military action.

Never appeasing those who threaten our nation and citizens.

Never negotiating with terrorists.

Defending ourselves against cyber threats.

Regular reviews of defence suitability and readiness.

Conflict resolution arbitration.

we are for change

Setting a percentage of our budget for domestic defence and security.

Setting a percentage of our budget for international peacekeeping and defence with no commitment to spend.

Investing in the physical and mental wellbeing of our service men and women.

Ensuring the safety and equipment suitability for all our service men and women.

Rewarding those who sacrifice themselves for our country.

Rewarding and honouring our ex service men and women.

Never forgetting the sacrifice others have made to maintain our freedom.

Honouring annually the sacrifices made by service men and women in times of war.

Providing university and further education scholarships for ex service personnel and their children.

Providing on going mental health support for current and ex service personnel.

Armed forces who are equipped, trained and ready to defend our nation and national interest.

Incentivising ex service personnel to take up positions in other national service roles.

Providing for the needs of those injured in the line of duty.

Providing schooling in line with the UK standard for all service families abroad.

Home Affairs

We Are For

Paid maternity and paternity leave.

Devolved responsibility for local issues.

Holding a mirror up to all government departments, industries, organisations and institutions to review efficiency and performance.

Reducing the influence of special interest groups.

Rebalancing the voice of the people against the voice of lobby and special interest groups.

Planning for the future in all departments.

Ten year and long term plans for all departments.

Proactive rather than reactive operations.

Services being fit for purpose.

Reviewing and removing failing services.

Working with industry where they can improve services, quality and costs.

Supporting working families with childcare opportunities and subsidised provision.

Filling government service contracts in Britain.

Improving public sector productivity through national and local private sector partnerships.

Results based payment in public sector contracts.

Encouraging local contributions and feedback in public sector contracts with service level rewards.

Excellent public sector services being run as private businesses and offered to other councils/bodies.

Encouraging innovation and public consultation in sector service provision.

Opening government tender contracts to businesses of all sizes by breaking up contracts into smaller, unique deliverables.

Adding timelines and penalties for government contracts.

we are for
change

Tight controls on public spending.

Value for money in the public sector.

Contracting public sector contracts to suitable private sector organisations.

Building the economy both locally and nationally.

Regional and national sovereign wealth similar to the Ontario teachers' Pension Plan.

Clear labelling of all foods including GM content.

Banning organisations which advocate hate, violence and terror.

Closing down and detain organisations and individuals who fund terrorism and extremism.

Protecting the identities of our citizens both in public and online.

Using technology to engage the electorate in the debate, legislation and law making.

Constituencies owning and maintaining their MP's Westminster residence.

Constituencies of equal size.

The right to recall politicians and replace them through bi-elections for serious misconduct.

The right and ability for individuals to introduce legislation for debate.

A cap on individual, institutional and organisational political and lobbying donations.

Open and accessible public accounts for all government departments and councils.

Publication of elected official and senior civil service expenses and gifts.

we are for
change

Business & Enterprise

We Are For

There never being an option not to work, without being supported by private means, and still maintain a high standard of living.

The fair representation of the lowest paid workers to the senior leaders within an organisation.

Supporting employers through difficult times.

Encouraging entrepreneurs and employers to create new jobs and employ new talent.

Providing support to those who invest in innovation, creativity, new technologies, new industries, growth, expansion and hiring new employees.

Incentivising foreign investment into businesses and employing within our country.

Incentivising employment.

Retailers (big and small),

Consumers, Products and Services.

Manufacturers, big and small, high and low tech, for consumers and business, both at home and abroad.

Services, to businesses, organisations, families, groups and individuals at home and abroad.

Competition, in all markets, all sectors, all industries and all areas of enterprise.

Supporting and encouraging innovation, creativity and new technologies and industries.

Investing in our future and future economies.

Free enterprise and entrepreneurship.

Supporting entrepreneurs with start up capital in return for interest or a profit / equity share

Business big and small, from sole traders to global corporations.

we are for change

Encouraging companies and markets to grow, develop and contribute positively to our economy.

Everyone being treated differently in the workplace in accordance with the contribution they make, the benefit and value they add, the skills they provide and the experience they bring.

Meritocracy.

Individuals being rewarded differently, in line with the value they add to an organisation and the contribution that they make.

The end of discrimination.

A minimum wage for all, that is high enough to ensure a quality of life, above the regional breadline, and leave some left over at the end of each month.

A minimum wage being greater in value than any support paid to those who choose not to contribute positively to society or our economy.

Thinking of new ways to develop business and markets.

Supporting industries to modernise during difficult economic times.

Public investment in private industry.

Sovereign investment and wealth.

Those who sell products or services in our country employing in our country.

Incentivising employment.

Punishing tax avoidance.

Apprenticeships and specialist career/vocational training.

Rewarding organisations who employ and retain benefit seekers and claimants.

Investing in creating high technology and green industry incubators and zones with government grants.

Rent control for private and commercial property set locally and independently.

Sovereign wealth involvement in SME financing.

Retail banks, savings and small business banks and investment banks.

Entrepreneurs, business leaders, shareholders, business owners, managers and directors.

Work & Pensions

We Are For

Ensuring that those who have dedicated a lifetime to contributing to our economy are rewarded and taken care of once they have retired.

Lifting pensioners out of poverty.

Taking care of those who have spent a lifetime contributing to our society and economy.

Caring for our elderly, disabled and infirm in their own homes where possible.

Supporting and providing respite for both official and unofficial carers.

Providing local and national support networks for carers.

Providing training and support for both official & unofficial carers.

Ensuring the state pension is enough to support a decent quality of life.

Means testing the state pension.

Winter fuel payments to lower income and net worth pensioners.

Allowances for those caring for the disabled, infirm or incapacitated.

All employees having access to a workplace pension to enhance their state pension.

Pensions linked to earnings.

The right to flexible working.

Rewarding business for taking on apprentices.

Encouraging business and educational collaboration and product development.

Encouraging intellectual property.

The national pension set above a living wage.

Ensuring all workers have access to an occupational pension.

Reducing the divide between public and private pensions.

we are for
change

Unemployment

We Are For

Those of us who can supporting those of us who, through no fault of their own, can't, be it through inability, incapacity or injury.

There never being an option to choose to live supported only by the government for those who can work.

There never being an option not to work and still have a high standard of living and luxuries.

Providing support to those who are not capable, through no fault of their own, to earn a living to support themselves.

Ensuring that support offers them a comfortable and dignified quality of life.

Providing temporary support to those who have been employed and who find themselves out of work.

Working with those individuals to help them find new, gainful employment as quickly as possible.

Attempting to ensure that employment is as relevant to the individual as possible.

Temporarily covering living costs for those who are out of work.

Ensuring that unemployment support is not greater than the amount that could be earned in an available job.

Terminating unemployment support if an individual refuses to take a job which is available, relevant and for which they are qualified.

Not providing support to the habitually unemployed or those who are unemployed through their own fault, negligence or deliberate action.

Not providing support to anyone caught, found guilty of or accused of committing a crime while receiving benefit.

Supporting the unemployed to start their own business with benefits backed loans

Rewarding businesses for employing apprentices, school leavers, young unemployed, those who are close to retirement and ex service personnel.

Minimum requirement in Maths, English and Computing before eligibility for Job Seekers Allowance or other unemployment benefit.

Taxation

We Are For

Fair taxation of all individuals and organisations.

Not punishing those who accumulate wealth from passing it on to their families, children and chosen beneficiaries.

Closing tax loop holes and punishing those who have intentionally benefitted from them.

Making taxation clearer, simpler and more efficient for all.

Tax free status/reduced tax status for required, key national service occupations.

Fair council taxation.

Reducing taxation for essential 'national service' employees.

Directing a percentage of key worker's tax directly into a private additional pension.

Simplifying individual and corporate taxation.

Tax revenue recycling.

Reducing the headline and small companies tax rates.

Closing loop holes to ensure that all corporate and business turnover generated in the UK is taxed.

Using fairer taxation to help Raise all our children and pensioners out of poverty.

Reducing National Insurance contributions for small businesses.

Removing tax for minimum wage earners.

A high threshold for inheritance tax.

Internationally competitive business taxation and regulation.

Encouraging enterprise by taxing fairly.

Rewarding employment through tax incentives.

Fair taxation for all individuals and organisations without loo holes.

Closing loop holes in taxation and back charging those who benefitted from them.

Reducing the burden of tax on the lowest income earners and taxing high earners more.

**we are for
change**

Value added tax levied on all, non essential, goods sold to the general public.

Value added tax levied on all goods and services provided by all individuals and organisations that turn over more than £50,000 per year for all products and services they provide.

Scaled value added tax for sole traders and small businesses.

Value added tax relief for start up businesses.

we are for
change

Benefits

We Are For

Supporting those who have fallen on hard times through no fault of their own.

Supporting those who are incapable of working due to physical or mental incapacity.

Reducing support to those who have rejected education.

Reducing and removing support to those who refuse to work when they are capable.

Seeking to recover all benefits given to those who are found guilt of receiving them fraudulently.

Regularly reviewing and reassessing eligibility for all benefits.

Encouraging all who can to work.

Benefits not being a replacement to work.

Benefits being a privilege not a right.

There being more incentive to work than claim benefits.

Benefits caps for all, relevant to family size and local cost of living.

Supporting local services though using capable benefit seekers.

Rewarding local businesses who employ a benefit seeker for an extended period of time.

Community project for benefits.

Ending zero hour contracts.

Work ending benefits.

Means testing fuel allowance for pensioners and young families.

Simplifying benefits and their eligibility.

The minimum wage for all.

Supporting working families more than benefits seeking families.

Winter fuel payments to lower income and young families.

Supporting low income workers to gain further or basic qualifications.

Ending benefit payments and prosecuting to those caught abusing the system.

**we are for
change**

Supporting the incapacitated.

Work for benefits programs, with community and social welfare being priorities for labour.

Removing benefits from those who refuse reasonable job offers or refuse to work.

Rewarding organisations who employ and retain benefit seekers and claimants.

Benefits backed loans for those who want to start their own business.

we are for
change

Local Affairs

We Are For

Fair council and local taxation to support local services.

Guaranteed rate relief for small and start up businesses.

Incentives for local expanding employers.

Devolved responsibility for local issues.

Regenerating brown fields and inner cities.

Fair council taxation.

Social enterprise, charities and voluntary groups leading public service delivery at a local level.

Social regeneration projects supported by local neighbourhood finance.

Grants for local voluntary and charitable organisations.

Communities working together on local issues.

Communities working together on local health issues.

Communities holding their police to account.

Local community organisers.

Utilising the civil service in civic service.

Encouraging youth participation in civic projects through specific rewards.

Using local councils to encourage local economic growth.

Ensuring super fast broadband is available to all addresses.

Devolving powers to communities that are relevant and appropriate to them.

we are for
change

Housing

We Are For

Home ownership.

Supporting first time buyers.

Helping everyone to own their own home.

Housing regeneration.

Supporting those who can afford to rent their home to buy their home.

Regulation of estate and letting agents.

Caps to the fees estate and letting agents can charge.

Brownfield site regeneration.

Reevaluating mortgage lending and mortgage rates.

Capping mortgage lifetime interest rates.

Helping essential workers to buy the properties they want to live in.

Rent control for private and commercial property set locally and independently.

Making it easier for those who can afford to pay the mortgage on a property to buy that property.

Cheaper life mortgages.

Building tariffs for green built development.

Building more affordable housing with strong transport links.

Reducing stamp duty for first time buyers.

Different stamp duty for personal, buy to let, commercial and institutional buyers.

we are for
change

Transport

We Are For

Reviewing the national speed limits both up and down to reflect improvements in technology and weight of traffic on our streets.

Zero tolerance of driving under the influence of drugs.

Ensuring migrants and immigrants are qualified and licensed to drive under and within UK law and the highway code.

Foreign registered vehicles being proven to be safe before being driven on UK roads.

Reducing the financial burden of commuting for low income earners.

Not punishing motorists though heavy taxation.

Reviewing our national speed limits.

Improving our road network and easing congestion black spots.

Increasing the efficiency of our rail network and increasing capacity.

Investing in public and mass transport systems.

Enabling and encouraging cycling as a form of commuting.

Incentivising business to cut work related travel and their carbon footprint.

Finding ways other than fixed speed cameras to make roads safer.

Testing for drug driving.

Making companies who dig up our roads relay whole road sections and fill pot holes.

Penalising congestion caused by companies digging up roads.

Linking fuel duty, oil company taxation and fuel price to stabilise fuel costs.

High speed transport infrastructure.

Using technology to increase rail and air capacity.

Targeting larger businesses and organisations on remote working and virtual working to reduce traffic and travel.

Reforming air passenger duty to make the UK a more attractive destination.

we are for
change

Reducing the carbon footprint of our public transport network.

Public and private investment in transport.

Compulsory speed awareness training for all new drivers.

Local road partnerships between councils, the police and the public.

we are for
change

Culture & Sport

We Are For

Cultural Diversity

Using national Lottery funding to support good causes in sport, the arts, education, heritage and care.

Publicly owned art displayed free of charge to the public that owns it.

Street art.

Bringing art and culture to communities and onto the street.

Engaging society in our heritage, culture and history.

Creating spaces in every community to celebrate the history and culture of that community.

Preserving our art, culture and history for future generations.

Using technology to engage the public in art, culture and our history.

Starting our children in different sports at school.

Involving professional sports teams and personalities in developing sports clubs in our communities.

Physical education in schools.

All children being active during the school day.

Challenging our children to be active.

Making time in every school day for active exercise.

Using our children to lead the country to be healthier.

Tackling inactivity and unbalanced diets as the root cause of obesity.

Teaching nutrition in school.

Supporting local sporting organisations and those who teach children to be healthier.

we are for
change

Youth

We Are For

Encouraging social participation and youth community involvement.

Rewarding youth participation in community projects.

Apprenticeships, specific job training and work experience programs.

Business and industry working in communities to develop and create opportunities for our youth.

Rewarding participation in youth community projects.

Rewarding businesses that employ school leavers and young workers full time.

Grants for local voluntary and charitable organisations that engage youth workers and volunteers.

Creating opportunities in business and society for youth participations.

Utilising new technology to engage our youth in the national debate.

Listening to the voice of youth.

Using grants and benefits backed loans to encourage young entrepreneurship.

Utilising local business people and specialists to mentor and guide young entrepreneurs and those who set out on their own.

Encouraging our youth to add value to their communities.

Encouraging our youth to follow careers into national key worker roles.

Helping our youth to buy their first properties.

Encouraging youth participation in civic projects through specific rewards.

we are for
change

Justice

We Are For

Trial by a jury of peers

Impartiality of the courts

Innocent until proven guilty

Victims rights.

Harsher punishment of habitual offenders.

Returning charging discretion to the police for minor offences.

Using technology to increase the efficiency of processing offenders in the street, custody and courts.

Border control linked to organised crime and security agencies.

Extending early deportation of foreign criminals including EU citizens.

Putting the rights of the victim at the centre of the criminal justice system.

Effective and professional legal aid.

New punishments for modern criminal issues such as carrying knives and cybercrime.

Strict sentencing guidelines for deliberate, habitual, sexual, hate, terror and violent crimes.

Protecting householder rights against intruders.

Protecting the identities of accused and victims from the public during trials.

Prisoner earnings being paid to their victims.

Educating the vulnerable to protect themselves against sexual exploitation.

A bill of rights.

Maximum time limits to hold and interrogate criminal and terror suspects.

A statue of limitations on all but sexual, violent and fatal crimes.

UK jurisdiction over UK issues.

we are for
change

Policing & Correction

We Are For

A standing police force.

A strong police presence on our streets.

Correctional facilities, prisons and psychiatric care.

Fines for those who use police time for preventable reasons like alcohol and drug related altercations.

Protecting the rights of the victims of crime.

Adequate and appropriate policing of the internet.

Independent courts and judicial services.

Sentencing guidelines for violent, fraudulent and sexual crimes.

Crime prevention.

Finding new ways to punish and rehabilitate criminals.

Preventative action against extreme behaviour.

Free and subsidised university and college education for those who enter front line police after qualifying.

Tax benefits for front line police officers and ex service personnel.

Reviewing and revising drug laws in respect to possession and personal use.

Reclassification of drugs.

Review and revision of the national speed limits.

Digital rights and online protection and policing.

The European arrest warrant and international extradition for violent, sexual, fraudulent, terror and hate crimes.

Deporting immigrant criminals.

Community orders.

Safe communities.

Community involvement in policing.

Imprisonment being about repaying a debt to society.

Offenders showing remorse before being released.

we are for
change

Custodial sentences to be about rehabilitation, education and correction.

Stricter and definite punishment for repeat offenders.

Minimum and Maximum sentences.

Offenders working to repay their debt.

Developing new ways to punish offenders other than custodial sentences.

Investing into keeping our street safe for all our citizens.

Involving communities and local business in their policing and service provision.

Working in communities to identify and remove the root causes of crime and antisocial behaviour.

Punishing in the community crimes committed in or against the community.

Putting common sense policing ahead of offender health and safety.

Returning charging discretion to the police for minor offences.

An unarmed society.

Using technology to increase the efficiency of processing offenders in the street, custody and courts.

Community based policing priorities.

Increasing the capacity of our prisons.

Strict discipline in prisons.

Supportive rehabilitation for those who choose it.

Drug and alcohol abstinence rehabilitation orders.

Specialist youth justice and rehabilitation.

Combatting the cause of antisocial behaviour at a local level.

Police officers in communities and visibly on the streets.

Incentivising ex service personnel to take up positions in policing and crime prevention.

Zero tolerance of drug driving offences.

Officers for crime investigation and officers for crime prevention.

Combatting the causes of crime at a local level.

we are for
change

Foreign Affairs

We Are For

Leading on the international stage.

Stamping out global terrorism, its supporters and incubators.

Using economic sanctions and potentially force against nations who harbour, shelter or encourage terrorism and extremism.

Exhausting all peaceable options before using force.

Never targeting civilians with economic or military actions.

Supporting those who seek freedom and human rights around the world.

Bringing to justice those who use torture and abuse human rights around the world.

Humanitarian intervention.

Strengthening our relationship with all nations around the world.

Expanding the reach and peaceful principals of the EU foundations.

Working with our allies.

Utilising the commonwealth to promote democracy, co-operation and goodwill among nations.

Preventing conflict, considered peacekeeping and peaceful resolution.

Working with Europe and other nations to boost and develop our mutual economies.

Protecting our citizens from all threats both foreign and domestic.

Protecting the weak from tyranny and oppression around the world.

Peacekeeping and impartiality around the world.

The active conversation of peaceful nations.

Uniting against a common enemy.

Negotiation and discussion as a first effort.

Exhausting negotiation & sanctions before taking military action.

Never appeasing those who threaten our nation & citizens.

A percentage of GDP for international peacekeeping without commitment to spend.

we are for
change

Europe & Immigration

We Are For

Free trade across borders.

Free movement of people across borders.

Citizens from across Europe contributing to our society and economy.

Removing those who are drains on our economy.

Ensuring no one can come to our country purely to claim benefits.

Those who come to our country contributing to our economy.

Denying the privileges of living in our country to those, not from our country, who do not contribute to our country and economy.

Deporting individuals and their families if they commit violent, sexual, fraudulent or serious crimes in our country.

All positive contributions to our economy.

Preventing entry to our country to those who have committed violent, sexual, fraudulent or serious crimes in their own country.

Removing those who fail to find work in our country after six months.

Imposing minimum standards of English for anyone wanting to gain permanent or long term residence in our country.

Putting an end to illegal immigration.

Detaining and deporting those who enter our country illegally.

Democratic reform of the European Parliament.

A European arrest warrant for violent, sexual, fraudulent and serious crimes.

A national vote on Europe.

Reforming the common agricultural policy.

Ending market distorting European subsidies.

Maintaining our currency and sovereignty.

we are for change

Securing our borders.

Ending Illegal immigration.

Detaining and deporting illegal immigrants.

Granting asylum to those who face persecution in their own country.

Deportation of violent, fraudulent, sexual or serious criminal migrants.

Migrants living within the confines of our laws.

Minimum standards of English for anyone wishing to be granted asylum, long term or permanent residence.

Strict visa limits and controls.

Incentives for attracting highly skilled immigrants to our country.

Easing entry into our country for our own citizens.

Protecting our citizens from persecution abroad.

Extending early deportation of foreign criminals including EU citizens.

Removing the passports of anyone who joins, fights for or financially supports terrorist or extremist organisations.

Deporting or denying entry to anyone who joins, fights for or financially supports terrorist or extremist organisations.

Limiting non EU migration.

Incentivising high value migration into the UK.

Completion of an English language test before migration is granted into the UK.

Border control linked to organised crime and security agencies.

Requiring all non UK citizens to have adequate health insurance for the duration of their stay in our country.

Charity and Aid

We Are For

A set percentage of GDP being assigned to international aid, without a commitment to spend.

Providing aid to those who need it most.

Providing aid directly to those who need it in the most suitable manor, never through governments or government agencies.

Supporting the work of aid agencies and charitable organisations.

Exploring all options of providing aid before committing to a specific path.

Targeting aid to where it is needed most in the manner it is most needed.

Raising the impoverished out of poverty.

Literacy for all.

Not allowing anyone to abuse or exploit the impoverished for their own gain.

A set percentage of GDP being assigned to disaster relief.

Lifting children out of poverty.

Making it easier to donate to local and national charities.

Relieving tax on charitable donations.

Determining where our aid is spent ourselves.

Working with NGO's to determine where and how aid and charity should be provided.

Being ready to provide immediate disaster relief around the world when required.

we are for
change

Environment

We Are For

Incentivising businesses to become carbon neutral or negative.

Developing new park, conservation and recreational spaces in communities.

Investment in developing Green Industries and innovations.

Carbon offset target and strict punishments for all energy and carbon dependent businesses.

Strict and punitive fines for breaches of environmental legislation.

Enabling and encouraging cycling as a form of commuting.

Incentivising business to cut work related travel and their carbon footprint.

Leading the world Green Economy.

Incentivised carbon neutrality locally and nationally.

Starting a race between organisations, industries, towns and councils to carbon neutrality.

Encouraging local environmental conservation project.

Local recycling targets.

Local waste to landfill targets.

Protecting and encouraging breeding schemes for endangered species.

Ending the illegal trade in wildlife.

Taking back our fishing waters.

Minimum standards of welfare in farming and food supply chains.

Protecting whales within our territorial waters.

Removing the blight of litter from our communities.

Creating and protecting woodland.

Solar panel installation on all public buildings.

Installing alternative energy sources in communities to benefit that community.

Supporting businesses and developers to install Green energy solutions.

Energy

We Are For

Reducing our dependence on foreign oil and natural gases.

Reducing our dependence and vulnerability to fluctuating fossil fuel markets.

Investing in new energy sources

Becoming energy independent.

Incentivising those researching, creating and generating new, sustainable and environmentally safe energy sources.

Becoming world leaders in energy.

Investing to become net exporters of energy.

Carbon offsetting.

Supporting and incentivising carbon neutrality and negativity.

Reducing dependence on foreign oil.

Investment and research into low carbon fuels.

Planning and building towards our sustainable and independent energy future.

Investing now in the infrastructure we will need for our future.

Linking fuel duty, oil company taxation and fuel price to stabilise fuel costs.

Capping energy company profits and linking to customer energy costs.

Investment into low carbon fuels.

Targeting energy companies to generate a percentage of all their power supply from Green sources.

we are for
change

The Future

We Are For

Having a long term economic, education, health and industrial plan, then working together to achieve it.

Funding for research in science, technology, engineering and medicines.

Leading the world in research, innovative and creative industries.

Centres for excellence in creativity, innovation, research, science and sports.

Networking research and innovation to improve development.

Challenging our citizens to innovate and develop creative solutions to our problems and opportunities.

Crowdsourcing ideas to improve our country, economy and society.

Networking business and industries to drive innovation and growth.

Incentivising collaboration across industries.

Investing now in the infrastructure we will need for our future.

Investing in our future and future economies.

Investing in creating high technology and green industry incubators and zones with government grants.

Thinking to the future and then investing to get there.

Preparing our children for the future workplace better.

Blue sky thinking.

Leading the world in technology, engineering, design, creativity, finance, service provision, manufacturing and retail.

Pushing new boundaries and forging new markets.

Leading the world in high tech manufacturing and exports.

Investing to be world leaders in new treatments, drugs and cures.

Preparing society for the future economy and workplace.

Working together for a better future.

This is not meant to be an exhaustive list of everything **we are for**. It is meant to stimulate the discussion, start to change the way we think as a country and change the way we frame the debate. The list is intended to grow, it is intended to build as we build as a country. It is intended to be a reference point.

If you have ideas or points you want to included then join us and tell us what you are for at

@What_we_are_for
#WeAreFor

Copyright © 2015 by @What_we_are_for
All rights reserved. This book or any portion thereof may not be reproduced or used in any manner whatsoever without the express written permission of the author, expect for the use of brief quotations in a book review.
First printed in the United Kingdom, 2015
ISBN: 978-1-326-20586-7

www.ingramcontent.com/pod-product-compliance
Lightning Source LLC
Chambersburg PA
CBHW070433180526
45158CB00017B/1161